ABOUT THE AUTHOR

A poet, mum, nurse and dog owner from West Yorkshire, Lindsey wrote her first poem, 'A forgotten doll on a child's windowsill', in her English A-Level class aged 18. She then wrote no poems for years. She restarted around a decade ago, writing them for family birthdays and to promote local businesses. She writes self-help poems or on any topic to order.

Lindsey has written each poem in this book with love, to simply brighten your day or help you through.

Lindsey Bust

A BOOK BY ITS COVER

AND OTHER POEMS

AUSTIN MACAULEY PUBLISHERS™

LONDON • CAMBRIDGE • NEW YORK • SHARJAH

A CIP catalogue record for this title is available from the British
Library.

ISBN 9781398430082 (Paperback)
ISBN 9781398430099 (ePub e-book)

www.austinmacauley.com

First Published (2021)
Austin Macauley Publishers Ltd
Level 37, Office 37.14D
1 Canada Square
Canary Wharf
London E14 5AA

To my wonderful family

POEMS

A Poem for the Stressed

It's awful when you're feeling stressed,
All you're doing is trying your best,
A balance is not there at all,
But it's what's required before you fall.
The trials of life have piled up high,
The amount of chores makes you sigh;
Pressures at work have become too great,
You're not sure when you last met up with your mates.
It's time to remember what life's all about,
What makes you smile, laugh and even shout.
Feelings, emotions might be stored up inside:
Try and embrace them, take it all in your stride.
Focus on good things, no matter how slight,
The road to recovery has no wrong or right.
Time to talk things over with someone who cares,
You may forget all your worries as you focus on theirs.
By practising mindfulness, your anxiety will lessen:
As you look around you and be aware of the present,
Ensure that you breathe and notice the sound,
As you inhale and exhale, a calmness will be found.
Write troubles down, then throw them away,
Or make notes of positives to read another day;
Take exercise, sleep well or rest plenty instead,
Make sure you are comfortable when you lie in your bed.
Smiling and laughter, it's true they're a tonic;
Try to remember you're human, not bionic.

Turtle

Not quite a tortoise but a turtle instead,

Still a hard shell with a slightly bigger head,

Carrying its load upon its back;

We as humans also do that,

Carrying worries, fears, responsibilities and homes.

Don't carry it all, not in one go:

Share your troubles with someone you know,

Don't take on others or the tower will grow,

Don't pile them up... don't build a wall,

Just stack what you need... don't need them all.

Dieting

Keeping trim in your forties can be tricky,
So I thought I'd write a little ditty.
Your body shape has altered so much,
The old look is in there, but filled out as such:
Years of eating a bit more than you need,
Meals and snacks on the go, sometimes just greed.
Your schedule makes it hard to fit in exercise,
But it must be done if you want to reduce your size.
If you've carried a baby and delivered a child,
To say it alters your body is putting it mild,
Though pram-pushing helps and fitting car seats is a strain,
This will help address all that weight gain.
Sleepless nights from teething or just a wet nappy,
Can mean snacking in the night just to keep yourself happy,
Exercises and being active can help with your plight,
Eat less, move more… shame you don't have more height!
There are so many diets out there to try,
Some seem reputable, others seem to lie.
You can do it yourself and save some cash,
Unless you like the recipes – it's a change from mash.
Think of your body like a machine:
Keep it topped up, it'll run like a dream.
Just put in what you need, too much will lead to fat,
Unless you burn it off, you could always do that.
The pounds will come off if you treat your body well,
But look after your health, respect yourself, as your body is just a shell.

Midlife Dating

If you find yourself single in the prime of your life,

Without a husband, a fiancé, partner or wife,

You shouldn't be dismayed – instead, have a ball!

Don't waste your time waiting for someone to call,

Take up those hobbies, join a group or a club:

At least you're not wasting your time down the pub.

Make yourself happy, do what you enjoy,

Spend quality time with your kids, whether girl or boy.

Work enough to manage, as long as you make ends meet,

Ensure you have enough left over so you can buy treats.

That's all you need in the grand scheme of it all:

Be open to life, don't build a big wall.

Live every day as if it's your last,

Tackle problems head-on, as time goes so fast.

Meet up with family and friends who help you through,

Be there for each other when happy or feeling blue.

Remember yourself, please don't forget who you are,

And you might just meet someone who's the best so far.

Bullying

If you're a bully, you know who you are:
You treat others badly and sometimes leave a scar.
It's your own jealousy and sadness that spurs you along –
Well, what you are doing is spineless and wrong.
Though rest assured, karma will strike:
In time something will happen which you don't like.
If you've been the victim and had bullies pick on you,
To be a success is the best you can do,
Go about your days with your head held high,
It's not easy to do, but at least give it a try.
Let things go over your head and believe that you can.
Bullies have been around for as long as man.
Let words fade away and if there's violence, report it now;
Tell someone you trust, you can cope and know how.
Get on with your life, live each and every day,
Don't let bullies affect you, don't let them have a say.
Rise above it and remember what you're worth,
You're better than they are and have been since birth.
Learn to say it, don't keep it inside,
It's your time to shine, fly, even glide.
They'll soon get bored and will simply move on,
Don't let anyone dull your sparkle or spoil your song!

Daisy the Dormouse Finds a Friend

Daisy the dormouse wanted more than anything to have her own friend,
She was quiet and shy and could never have guessed how it would end!
She looked all around her at others she met,
Yet little did Daisy know that some were a threat.
There was Felix the fox with his black shiny nose,
He was clever and cunning, so he wasn't the one that she chose.
Beatrice was a butterfly who flapped quickly and seemed almost on edge,
She wasn't in one place long enough to chat, settling finally on a hedge.
She then studied Wilson, a wise old owl:
With his large eyes and neck that turned, he could spot others on the prowl.
There was Fran the falcon who was strong yet calm;
With her big wingspan and keen eyes, she too could cause harm.
Then she came across Colin, a crocodile with large white teeth:
He lives near the lake, sneakily sliding into the water, hiding underneath.
Sam the squirrel was the last one she studied,
A bit shy like her as he quickly scurried.
He had purpose and was busily gathering nuts to store away,
Daisy thought he'd make a good friend – at last she'd found someone with whom she could play.
The pair did get on and loved playing together,
The dormouse and the squirrel were friends for what seemed like forever.
However, Daisy had discovered herself the best thing about this rhyme:
She was strong and smart and could rely on *herself* until the end of time.

Poems by Lindsey x

Part of Life

Hello anxiety, I didn't need you today:
Sometimes you're gone, other times you stay.
You have your uses and are part of life,
In my stomach on occasion you cut like a knife.
It's best to embrace you, take it all in my stride,
As when I call you, you're there waiting inside.
I try not to worry if I feel you too much,
You're on my side but I don't always want you as such.
If you come for no reason, I don't get alarmed
As it's part of living, so you do me no harm.

Keep Flying

Just like a baby bird learning to fly,
Circling the nest and then flying high,
The trick is to keep flying all throughout life,
Try not to touch down when there's trouble or strife.
By all means stop to refuel or eat food,
But try and keep airborne, whatever your mood.
This skill that you've learned will keep you going forever:
The most simple of things is a bird and its feathers.

Mums

Mums are awesome, always there,
Ready with a hug to show they care,
Full of fun, good at making things better,
There if they're needed with your favourite sweater,
Good at cooking, mending and sewing,
Friendly, funny and very outgoing,
Always there with tea in your favourite cup –
Also mum's taxi when you need picking up.
They might be the breadwinner and have a career:
Let's hear it for mums with a great big cheer.

Mindfulness and Moving on

All the hurt has gone away:
Time to welcome a brand new day.
The events of the past have left a scar,
But look forward now and you'll go far.
Don't dwell on what was and what might've been,
The grass back then wasn't any more or less green.
Your time is now, so smile and breathe,
Your memories must be cherished but painful ones, leave.
Your future is exciting: hold no regrets from before,
Be happy, look forward to the future and go through that door.
As one chapter ends another will start:
Be hopeful and grateful and follow your heart.
Some friends come and go, others will stay,
Look for the beauty and promise in each new day.
Each relationship is special and shapes who you are:
Be grateful for what you have and you'll go far.
Learn new skills, cherish ones you hold dear;
Knowledge is power, that much is clear.
You're never too old to start something new,
You don't know 'til you try, so you know what to do!
Remember to work but also to play
And wake up excited at each new day.

New Year

The end of the year is drawing near,
It's time to reflect on what you hold dear:
Your family, friends, colleagues and pets,
Take a look back in time with no regrets.
Each month that has passed holds memories clear,
Celebrations, achievements make your heart full of cheer.
As New Year approaches what is important, it seems,
Is not your possessions but hopes and dreams,
So welcome the next chapter with your arms open wide,
Remember what's important and simply enjoy the ride.
The end of the year is approaching fast,
Stay in, go out… make sure you have a blast.
Not long now until New Year is seen:
Focus on where you're going and remember where you've been.

Dear Santa...

I've been really good this year,

My behaviour has made everyone cheer.

I've been helpful and kind and worked hard too,

Thinking of others in all I do.

I have left some supper for you to enjoy,

Also some ideas about my favourite toy.

There's a snack for the reindeers to keep them strong,

As they use lots of energy to pull the sleigh along.

Choices

The choices you make makes you you:
We all have choices in all we do.
The road could be a positive or a negative one,
But life's a journey, when all's said and done.
Choose wisely when you decide each path:
A good move will make you smile or laugh.
Our time on Earth is not that long,
To feel so good cannot be wrong.

Christmas Message – the Robin Is Seen

Autumn leaves wonderful colours everywhere,
The trees are transparent and almost bare.
Halloween has been with the trick-or-treaters,
Then bonfire night with its big flames to heat us.
People light fireworks, some with a loud bang,
We await Christmas with a wreath which we hang.
Presents are bought and a big mighty feast,
We remember the story with a star from the East.
Soft white snow can fall on the ground,
Carol singers make such a magical sound,
Gritters and snow ploughs are put to the test,
But it's time with loved ones I like best.
The robin is seen singing its song,
Saying that New Year won't be that long!

World Kindness Day

The tonic for feeling stressed is being kind –
Well, it is as regards our body and mind.
In a world where everyone strives for the best,
It's easy to forget yourself and have no time to rest.
A simple smile is infectious and translates across the earth;
Meet stress with kindness, show someone what they're worth.
Only when you're kind to yourself will kindness spread around,
Actual peace and calmness only then can be found.

A Book by Its Cover

People tend to see what they want to see,

When they are judging you or me:

A book isn't always the same as its cover,

The outside doesn't reflect how it feels being another.

We all have chapters, a verse, even lyrics,

A side that's OK and that's what it mimics.

There's a side that struggles like a swan with busy feet,

Always remember this with everyone that you meet.

World Mental Health Day

October the tenth is dedicated to Mental Health:
To have a happy mind is happiness itself.
When all is good and a balance is found,
Everything is level, our feet are firmly on the ground.
If trials and tribulations are proving too much,
The brain gets too full and simply overflows as such.
Call it a bucket or maybe a sieve,
Everything goes in it for all the time that we live;
The sieve has holes, life events pass through,
But the holes can get blocked for lots of reasons too.
Humans have developed in science as such,
But in mental health knowledge we haven't grown as much.
The brain is like a bucket which empties through a tap:
It can get too full, we should be aware of that.
Talking over problems will help reduce the strain,
And prevent too many things piling up in your brain.

Spider's Web

A spider spins a new web every time,

Individual and unique with every criss-cross and line,

Delicate yet strong, a place to catch food,

So the spider can feed off it and provide for its brood.

They look beautiful in winter all covered in frost,

But don't underestimate that insect, for it is the boss!

A Brand New Day

A brand new day has begun:

Spend some time having fun!

We cannot control everything, some things are left to chance;

Live life, love, and remember, there's always time to dance.

Worrying or overthinking changes nothing but your state of mind,

Letting go, not holding it all in, is more beneficial, you'll find.

Women

March the 8th is National women's day:
About empowering women, what can I say?
Women over time have shouldered a great deal,
Caring for others, not always how they feel.
They may raise children or they may not,
Or care for a relative with everything they've got,
Often counselling and nurturing yet carrying guilt,
If they put themselves first or maybe spill some milk.
Mending, cleaning, washing and cooking dinners,
The modern woman may have a career and also be breadwinners.
Body and self image may have also been a stress,
Whether long hair, short hair, trousers, skirt or dress.
Skinny jeans and leggings can be worn by most,
If a long top is needed, don't be afraid to boast.
Footwear varies from flats, heels or boots,
Hair can be dyed, not forgetting those roots.
Eyebrows now are trendy and contouring all the rage,
Go with what makes you feel good, not what's right for your age!

Pebbles

Each pebble thrown creates a ripple,
Everything can sometimes tipple;
The ripples form circles which grow in size,
Which eventually fade away, you'll realise.
A new pebble thrown will cause the same,
It's beginning to feel just like a game.
The circles vary in size and length,
Pebble or boulder determines its strength.
Each ripple runs its natural time span,
The water is still again just like it began.

Stepping Stones

Each stepping stone leads to the next:
It's easy to sometimes become perplexed.
Try your best and always use your head,
Don't worry about tomorrow, focus on now instead.
With each step your confidence will grow,
And you'll just know the way to go.

Inner Strength

If the mountain feels too big to climb,

Try and remember this little rhyme:

You're stronger than you think, more resilient than you know,

Just put one foot in front of the other and you will conquer it so.

Make the Most

Learn to accentuate all that you have got,
Don't try and be something that you're not;
Always be the best version of who you are,
Rather than zoning in on a blemish or a scar;
Make the best of your eyes, whether green or maybe blue,
Wear your hair long or short, try a hat or two;
You might have nice hands or simply lovely skin,
If not, don't dismay; you may be tall or thin,
Stature doesn't matter, you could be short but feel six feet,
Wear a smile and you'll go far, each day will be a treat.

Be Still

Sometimes it's nice to just sit and be still,
When celebrations are over and you've had your fill.
Let your mind settle and your tired body rest;
Keep snuggled and cosy in a lovely thermal vest;
Eat up leftovers, watch a film, take a walk,
Listen and look around; if you feel the need, talk,
Look up at the skies, at the paths where planes have been.
Focus on this time, the best moment that you've seen.

Friends

Some are there for a reason,
Some are just there for a season.
Some are there during the fall,
Some are there through it all.
Some join you for summer or spring,
Some are just there doing their thing.
Some are there simply forever,
Some are around for whatever.
Some are around just for the best,
Some are there for all the rest.
Some are there in their time of need,
Some are there to take the lead.
Some are there when things are fine,
Some are there until the end of the line.

Poems by Lindsey x

Others

You cannot change anyone else,
So focus instead upon yourself.
We all have habits that irritate others,
It's no good blaming your experiences or another,
We all can alter if we truly desire.
Our strength within is like a roaring fire,
Better yourself like a finely tuned guitar,
Let others do their thing and you'll go far.

People

Some come into your life forever,

Some just for a day and others never.

Some have a fleeting glance,

Others may lead to a romance.

Some are family, some are friends,

Or it might be a pet on who you depend.

Some you know for a very long time,

A month or a year, which is also fine.

Some are there for a purpose and appear at a difficult time,

Others might call on you, it could be you ensuring they are fine.

In this rich tapestry which is woven with patterns and lovely colours,

Be mindful that people come and go, it's about being there for each other.

Body

My body usually serves me well,
Albeit just a shell:
It takes me places, breathes in and out,
Enables me to sing or shout.
It means that I can work or play,
Support myself and enjoy each day,
It carried a child and delivered my son:
The circle of life has then begun.

Modern Life

If I wanted to tell people everywhere I go,
I'd meet up with them and tell them so:
My phone comes up with where I've been,
Asking me how it was and who I've seen.
Take a walk outside in some lush green grass,
Speed up, then slow down – it's good not to dash.
Look up from your screens, iPads, phone, satnavs,
Your PC, your TV, now all must-haves.
Look around, listen, stare up at the sky;
It's good to be still whilst the world rushes by.

Close to a Flame

If you've been challenged and had your fingers burned,
It's easy to forget all you've learned,
Whenever you feel to be getting close to a flame,
And you're frightened of ever getting burned again.
Remember your knowledge and how strong you can be,
You can put out that fire and set yourself free.

Look After Yourself

Don't be a squirrel, be an owl instead,
With its strong sturdy wings and a turn-around head.
An owl is wise but respected too;
It can see in the dark, it knows what to do.
Some are scorpions with a sting in their tail:
Don't be a cunning fox or a slow snail.
Be quick to respond but don't react,
Look after yourself, make a pact,
To do what you can with all you have got,
But be yourself, don't be something you're not.

Where You Should Be

When life doesn't map out as you expected –
Maybe you lost your job or have been somehow rejected –
The path you're now on is different and new,
But I promise it could be a great journey too.
Each twist and turn, corner or bend,
You could never guess life on this road it would send.
Don't be afraid but enjoy the change with glee,
This new direction will take you to where you should be.

Missing Piece

When you lose someone close or maybe something,

There's a void, or a hole it may bring,

Like a jigsaw puzzle which isn't complete,

You could get good wishes from others you meet,

Find a distraction to help you fill that gap,

A hobby, an interest something you're good at,

A new friendship, a course, a career change or use your voice.

Time is a healer: you do have a choice.

That missing piece of the jigsaw can be filled,

And those who matter most will be thrilled.

It's not that you've forgotten who or what has gone,

But you've found a new normal so you can go on.

Treading Water

When you're treading water, no sign of a float,
There is just one thing you ought to note:
You've been here before and it didn't last,
Remember how strong you've been in the past.
Simply float or swim front or back crawl,
You've done them with ease, you know them all.
Keep your head up, use your legs and arms,
Look around you, remember your lucky charms.
Focus on others, look after them too;
Things will find perspective, they always do.

Be Kind

You don't know what people have endured before today,

Please be kind in everything you do or say.

Layers of sorrow and of grief,

There lies a diamond underneath.

Like an orange and its peel,

Take off the hard skin and reveal

The inner goodness, nice and sweet:

Be kind to everyone you meet.

Good to Know

With every child a seed is planted:
It's easy to take health for granted.
Nourish and water this seed you've sown,
Spend time and listen, then notice it's grown.
It has roots which go deep and branches to reach out,
But giving them wings is what it's all about.
Gaining knowledge and also to discover,
To have family values and care for each other,
Expressing feelings and knowing yourself,
Is much more valuable than excessive wealth.
Enough for shelter, warmth and food,
And whatever else takes your mood.
Teach them to be someone good to know,
Rather than be well known, with all on show.

Magical Things

Magical things do happen in this world in which we live:
Each child who's born, every flower that grows, and presents that we give.
Laughter and smiling, excitement, simply having fun,
Each and every day has promise – and it's only just begun!

Social Media

Everyone is online these days! It's true it can be useful,
But social media can be a pain and sometimes even brutal.
Take it all with a pinch of salt, don't believe everything on there;
People dress up their moments and they decide what to share.
Whatever you post can be seen by most, whether pictures or what you say:
You never know, you might regret it if it bites you back one day.

No Stone Unturned

Put to practice all you've learned,
Make sure you leave no stone unturned:
Skills from college or what you've been through,
Use them all in all you do,
Courses you've done and people you've met,
Pursue all your dreams, don't have regret.
The exam of life is hard, you know,
But study well and far you'll go.
Experience too counts for a lot,
Don't be afraid to show all you've got.

Nursing

Being a nurse is not very easy:
You cannot be one if you're a little bit queasy!
Looking after others is the aim of the game,
Whether old or young, treat them all the same,
All walks of life, all classes and races,
Helping people and putting smiles on their faces.
An honest, uplifting and challenging life choice,
Looking out for others and ensuring they have a voice.
An advocate caring for those you hold dear,
Who's chosen to make a difference as their career.

How You Feel

What you think is how you feel:
Concentrate on something real,
Where you are, your breath, the sound,
Noises and smells all around.
Negative thoughts make you feel bad;
Don't procrastinate about things you had,
Focus on now and look to tomorrow,
Don't look back, try not to wallow.
There's always hope, so don't dismay,
Don't let yesterday spoil today.

Fly

How wonderful to fly like a bird,
To float through the air above all the world,
To feel the breeze, be as light as a feather,
Exposed to the elements, experience all weather,
No worries or cares, fly with your family and friends,
Simply build your own home until the very end.

Lovely Things

Hold a crystal in your hand,
Wiggle your toes in soft white sand,
Walk barefoot through lush green grass,
Meet up with friends and have a laugh,
Blow a dandelion clock to tell the time,
You could even write a little rhyme,
Play hopscotch or even elastics,
Collect conkers, do some magic…
All of these make you feel whole,
Treat your senses, cherish your soul.

A Forgotten Doll

I'm homeless, got nowhere to live,

Like a lump of flour that won't go through the sieve.

Nobody cares, no one wants to know,

I have no job or money, so

I'm homeless, got no home,

My life is like a glass of wine alone.

People walk past, everyone stares,

Nobody stops, they don't care.

I live on the streets, probably always will,

I'm like a forgotten doll on a child's windowsill.

I need to walk through the city and be accepted.

Is this life? It's not what I expected.

China Cup

We all resemble a China cup:
It's not how we fall, but the way we get up.
Trials and tribulations leave a scar,
But once it's mended you can still go far.
You may have a weak spot that isn't as strong,
But with time and attention you can still go on.
Cracks are simply character that make us unique,
Which could be hidden by a pattern or the way we speak.
Resilience is crucial and confidence is key:
Experience gives us grit to be the person that you see.

Dogs

Our little dog is half Bichon Frise,

She leaps onto the bed or sofa with ease.

She pushes doors open with her small shiny nose,

She sometimes needs grooming when her soft fur grows.

Part of the family with my son, her and me,

She likes to sit on your lap when you're watching TV.

When she's emptied her bowl, she'll drop it at your feet:

For a very small dog, she has plenty to eat!

She tells you, 'I'm hungry and could eat a bit more,'

And when you come in from work, she greets you at the door.

She likes to snuggle and loves being cosy,

She barks at the window, some might think she's being nosey.

It's true what they say about man's best friend:

Cheerful, respectful and loyal to the end!